It Don't Make Sense not to Trust God!!!

By

Dr. Toni Boulware Stackhouse

It Don't Make Sense Not to Trust God!

Dedication

I dedicate this book to my husband, Elder Samuel A. Stackhouse III, who I love dearly and with whom I have learned faith on another dimension because of this journey we have shared for the last two years. My husband is my miracle man and I thank God for his enthusiasm and will to live LIFE against the odds. He has been determined to push beyond the limitations in search for a new life and God has exceeded his expectations. He has given so much encouraging love and laughter through this storm! His desire to love and encourage people despite his own challenges has been nothing short of amazing. In life you only get to know what you are made of in tough times and I am understanding more how God has blessed me with Sam. Although unexpected, this journey has created in us a great union that makes for a great foundation and we can only imagine where life will lead us. I'm so excited about our future because I know it is filled with greatness. The enemy camc for us and we persevered by the grace of God. I'm so excited to do LIFE with Sam on God's terms.......after this.....it don't make sense not to trust God.......after YOU God!!!!

Acknowledgements

First I thank God who is simply amazing, and of course without him there is nothing to write about. He has been my rock helping me to maintain balance in an unsteady place and for that I am eternally grateful. Next I would like to thank my family who has got to be the best family in the world. They have stood with Sam and myself since August 23, 2017, Day 1, and still continue to stand with us. And this journey has been long and hard. My parents are true gems, loving and caring for Sam as their own son; doctors and therapy appointment, pick-ups and drop-offs to Richmond. My daughter and son son, who rock, make sure I am well taken care of. My daughter ensured that I was never alone at the hospital and when things got tough she reached out to other family members for assistance with transportation rotation for Richmond. My sister and brother-in-law walked in faith with us, encouraging and pushing. Sam's mother, Stephanie Walters, Aunt Theresa and Uncle George for allowing Sam to visit while I was working. Uncle Richard and all other family members and friends for their prayers. We want to thank our covering, Bishop Ronald G. and Pastor Angela King for their prayers and support and guidance during this ordeal! We also want to thank Archbishop Ralph L Dennis and Lady Deborah Dennis and family for the prayers and support! We have had a host of family and friends praying us through this journey and we could not have made it without you all and I pray God's blessings on your life for blessing us!!!

Table of Contents

Introduction

One day I was struggling mentally and emotionally to make sense of all we were going through. I was vacillating between wondering why this was transpiring in my life and how it would all end. Also pondering if I could do what God was calling me to do and at this particular time in life. I was questioning how God was going to do what he had promised. Also wondering if we would experience the move of God that we so desperately desired. And if it had not happened so far, would God even perform this miracle for us. And then it happened, it came to me in a still small voice, just as clear as day, but emphatically, "It don't make sense not to trust God!" Then I came to myself and realized that was indeed the case. How could I not trust a God who has been faithful to me all my life? During that moment I reminisced about all of the things that God had already performed in my life up to this point. It was in that very moment I understood how foolish it is not to trust a God who is and will forever be faithful to his children.

Sometimes we get caught up in the minutia of things trying to figure out just how God is going to do what he has promised to do. And we need to understand this is not our concern. Our only responsibility in the matter is to trust God, which requires us to move forward with our part in what he has planned for us. Knowing that he has his part under control, even when it seems like nothing is happening or moving in the direction we want to go in. God is faithful and his track record precedes him and he needs no help from us, other than the faith and obedience required to experience a performance from an almighty God.

So my quandary initially was whether to move forward in ministry now or to wait until my understanding of full manifestation of promise occurred. Then I realized my understanding of full manifestation is faulty at best. God is looking for obedience despite how it looks, regardless of what we are facing. We have to decide to have the kind of faith in God that supersedes our feelings. Feelings change and we need to ensure that we are in control of our emotions lest we allow ourselves to miss God and the opportunity to have him move in our lives.

This book is about manifesting in the earth regardless of the challenges that may exist. We are all called to manifest in the earth what God has placed in us before we were formed in the womb. You will read something in this book that will encourage you to be who God created you to be without hesitation and resistance!

Because it don't make sense not to trust God!!!

Chapter One: It don't make sense!

God extended his faithfulness to the earth long before we were placed into existence. This display of love in action occurred when he spoke things into existence during creation and those things are still manifesting in the earth today. In Genesis 1 it says that the earth was without form and was void. God spoke light into darkness and there was light. He then separated the light and darkness into day and night. We live with the light he spoke and do so without thought for it; however, we depend on it occurring. Without the light there would be chaos across the land, but because he spoke it, we have it and we have the assurance that it will occur without incident.

It is also no coincidence that during the creation story God created us in his image and likeness, meaning we resemble him. God is spirit and if we are created in his image and likeness, it is our spirit man made in his image and likeness. So spiritually we should be like him. We should be able to speak things into existence and them manifest. Our being in the earth should resemble him through the Holy Spirit who is our helper in the earth. The Holy Spirit helps us to manifest God in the earth realm. The plans of God happen through the use of his people. We are his hands and feet yielded to his desire when we surrender and submit to him.

Everything God has set into motion functions without hesitation or delay but the manifestation of the sons of God. Every day the sun rises and every evening it sets regardless of the weather conditions. Even when it is cloudy or a rainy day the sun still rises and sets. When I was younger I thought when the weather was rainy or cloudy that the sun was not active at all that day. One day it was raining and I was listening to the weather forecast and the weather man gave the times that the sun would rise and set and I was amazed. I had no idea prior to that moment that when the weather was adverse that the sun was still going to rise and set. Of course it was going to rise and set. God created it to do so regardless of the conditions. And so it is that when God created us to be in the earth realm, it was not based on conditions but rather in spite of them. However we sometimes struggle with this and because we do, something is lacking in the earth and it is waiting for us to manifest!

Yet creation is moaning and groaning for the sons of God to manifest!!! The earth needs us to be who God created us to be, point blank, without hesitation and resistance. God created us to be a solution to a problem in the earth and that is why the earth is groaning for the solution to the problems that exist. People need the salvation of God, healing and deliverance from the wickedness of the enemy and for some of us, this is not our focus because we live with a certain level of freedom in God. We have to remember when we were desperate for God and how he used someone to rescue us from whatever was ailing us. Now someone else is in a desperate situation crying out to God for help and God has placed in us resolution to those living in a dying world and we have no sense of urgency to move on the behalf of others.

Why are we not becoming who God designed us to be? Why do we allow our external conditions to affect us in this way when we have been given the outcome as victors? With God we always win and knowing this we sometimes struggle in just becoming. Is this a trust issue? We say we have faith in God and that he is faithful, however our actions rarely line up with this declaration? We have to understand that faith is not only declarations but it must be accompanied with acts of obedience that directly line up with what we believe. Faith is not about having God meet our self-motivated desires, but about the plan God has for our lives. We want God's plans to conform to our agenda and that affects the manifestation of what we are believing for. The bible instructs us to seek first the kingdom of God; then and only then will he add all those other things to us. {*Matthew 6:33*} We want things first, then we will consider what God desires from us. God had plans for our lives prior to our birth and we are so busy presenting him with our agenda that we miss the mark of what is at stake when we fail to manifest who we are to be in the earth. Yes a problem remains unresolved; people are waiting on us to manifest and that means their prayers, needs and desires go unmet until we decide to become.

How is creation still trusting God and in alignment with his will and we are a part of his creation and we fail to manifest daily and for some a whole lifetime. Imagine not becoming who God created you to be for your lifetime. We make all kinds of excuses explaining the reason we can't be who God has created us to be. While those people we are supposed to have an impact on continue to suffer, waiting on us to decide whether we are going to be obedient to the mandate of God on our lives. If you were waiting on God to answer your prayer request and the person he wanted to use to manifest your answer was struggling, making excuses as to why they could not respond; that would be frustrating for you. Well the people you are supposed to have an impact on are waiting for you to decide that now is the time to manifest. We are God's hands and feet in the earth. He uses his children to accomplish his desire in the earth and some of us struggle for various reasons to become what he desires us to be. For most of us, we know what God desires from our lives; however, we struggle with fear on various levels that prevents us from moving in that direction.

What if the sun made excuses about why it could not rise or set, what Chaos would that create in the earth? Or the moon decided not to shine at night, what darkness would befall the earth? God saved the earth from darkness and provided light and automatically it happens at his command. Well imagine that is the same kind of chaos being created in the earth now because we will not just be who God created us to be. If the sun does not rise there would be darkness across the earth in the same way that we see darkness in the lives of people because we fail to operate the way God created us to.

Even when there are clouds in the sky, the sun still rises and sets. One thing we never have to worry about is whether there is going to be daylight. Even if the sun doesn't shine, it rises. That speaks to the faithfulness of God and his provision for us. He has given us everything we need in the earth to be successful and the continuous excuses we use make God look like he's not faithful to those who are waiting on the manifestation of their answer. This is absolutely far from being true. God has a plan of salvation for all of us and that is not just about securing a place in heaven. This speaks to his plan to save us from the plans of the enemy, even when the enemy is ourselves. Yes he wants to save us from ourselves too. It is our way of thinking that causes us to delay in what he is calling us to do.

In the same manner that God has spoken to the sun and the moon and given it direction on what to do, he has also spoken to us in conversation about who we are to become. Words to the prophet Jeremiah were, "Before I formed you I knew you." In essence God is saying he knew us, I know what I purposed you to be and then I placed you in your mother's womb for you to enter the earth and become just that. So then if this is in fact the truth then why when God has spoken to us to do some things we make all kinds of excuses about why we cannot fulfill the assignment. Surely if the sun can rise and set in adverse conditions this is an indication to you and I that things will not always be perfect but that does not preclude us from being who God created us to be. In fact we need to use those challenges as motivation to be determined to become who he created us to be. Usually when we push forward we find that those conditions eventually subside and had we not moved we would have missed an opportunity to not only become who God created us to be, but to see him deliver victory to us. We always win and obedience to God's plan for our lives secures that victory for sure!

The adversary's desire is to prevent us from becoming who God has created us to be. So he will try to place obstacles in our way. We should actually use that as our motivation to keep moving forward regardless of what he may try to throw our way because we are not ignorant to his devices. His schemes have already been revealed to us; his desire is to steal, kill or destroy and sometimes we allow him to do that without even a fight. It is almost as if we do not value the treasure God has placed in us. We have to begin to see the value of God creating us and his intent. And once we discover this purpose we should seek hard after it because that is where we find the greatest victories of life. It is shameful when people live and die, never having scratched the surface of purpose for their lives. This world is full of people wandering aimlessly, not having any idea of where or how to seek purpose for life. For some of us our purpose is helping to point people in God's direction in search of his intent for creating them. Heaven forbid we miss this opportunity to assist those in becoming.

The earth is groaning for you to be who God created you to become and someone is waiting on you!!!!

Chapter two: Wisdom and knowledge

No matter what profession we find ourselves in, whether in the marketplace or ministry inside the church, ultimately it is the grace given to us from God that sustains us. When we submit the very gifts and talents he has given us back to him, he blesses whatever we put our hands to with multiplied fruit. It is foolish for us to believe that within ourselves, outside of him, we have all the answers and know the right moves in all situations. This is not the case. Seeking God in all things is crucial; not just in the difficult things though certainly in those times we are sure to find him along with what we need. Sometimes what we need from God is different from what we are seeking; however when we trust him we determine that they are the same. God knows what we need and when we need it and once he has released that to us we find contentment in that even when we had no prior understanding of that being the need. Trusting and seeking God in the hard places can be challenging but remaining focused on the goal will help us stay on the path where God is leading. When we do not have all the answers to our questions in hard times that can cause us to have anxiety, allowing fear to step in and in the panic of not knowing, we stress instead of relying on an all knowing God who will not fail his children. In trusting in him, we find peace even in hard times. His peace gives us assurance that he is involved and that gives assurance that this too will work out for our good. Nothing compares with the peace of God and knowing he has us in the palm of his hands. Nothing is a surprise to him and nothing can catch him off guard; this being the case, when we find that we are surprised by anything we should seek after him. God has all the answers we need and all we have to do is ask him.

The bible encourages those who lack wisdom to ask for it. {*James 1:5*} We all lack wisdom without seeking the wisdom that comes only from an all knowing God. There is no wisdom or knowledge that supersedes the knowledge and wisdom of God! This is absolutely the truth. The bible declares that God is all knowing {*Isaiah 43:13-14*} which means he operates from a place of knowing how everything will unfold and even the ending. This being the case we operate with very little knowledge in comparison. When we make plans we do so from a blind position. God's plan for us has no limitations; he sees the entire picture. That is why it is key for us to trust him, knowing that he has more knowledge and wisdom than we have. When we find ourselves in situations that we are unsure of it is in our best interest to seek him and the wisdom and knowledge he wants to bestow upon us. When we operate in this manner we have peace that goes beyond our understanding and we are led to move in the direct path into which God is guiding us.

God absolutely cannot be blindsided. So our trust in him is an absolute necessity. As we yield our will over to him and learn more about him, that trust increases and our faith is exercised which matures us as well. As this occurs we should be moving as we are led by God through his wisdom and knowledge being assured that he has us where he wants us to be in that particular moment in time. Nothing just happens. God is very much intentional about what he does and what he allows. Purpose can be found through it all for a surrendered vessel earnestly seeking to know God more intimately, which should be our goal. When we try to operate outside of God's wisdom we find ourselves in situations and circumstances with no real direction for his intent. We have to understand that God has a plan based on his wisdom and knowledge and we are not able to discern that outside of him. Nor should it be our desire to do so......

Chapter three: When God interrupts...

When God interrupts our regularly scheduled plans for our lives things can get interesting for sure. When an interruption ensues in the life of a believer it can be one orchestrated by God for a redirection. It takes spiritual discerning to ascertain what is transpiring and that will determine how to approach the interruption.

On Wednesday, August 23, 2017 it appeared for all intents and purposes to be a normal day for my husband and me. When I woke up, I realized he was still at home, which was not normal for him, because he usually left for work before I did. He said he was tired and he was going to rest and go to work later. So I proceeded to get dressed and before leaving for work he told me he would call when he left the house. I noticed the time was getting late and I hadn't heard from him, so I called him. When he answered he immediately laughed out loud, saying after he took his shower he sat back on the bed and fell back to sleep. So we both laughed and he said again, that he would call when he left the house. He did call around noon to say he was going to work until 8 p.m. My husband was tired. The week prior to this day we had just returned from Jamaica, celebrating our second wedding anniversary. And the weekend after that we flew to Missouri to drop my nephew off at college, returning home Sunday night. Our usual practice when returning home from being away is to take another day off just to rest, but this time we did not because of some pressing task for work. So we returned to work immediately, although we were both tired.

We talked several times throughout the day which is usual for us and all appeared normal. I remember leaving work early that day because I was exhausted. When I arrived home I started washing our travel clothes and then took a nap. While I was in the laundry room washing clothes, Sam sent a text asking what was for dinner, but I did not realize he had done so. Receiving no response, he called my phone at approximately 8:07 p.m. He asked if I received his text and I responded that I had not received it. He was inquiring about dinner and I informed him that we were having leftovers. He told me he was on the way home and if anyone knows my husband that could still have been hours later because he was likely to run into someone he knew and talk to them for hours. Or he could meet someone new and talk to them for hours. So I was like okay. Now during this conversation there is no sign of anything being wrong with my husband at all. It appeared to be a normal conversation.

So shortly after the phone conversation I heat up dinner and await his arrival. At about 9 p.m. I received a call from my sister in law, Sam's brother's wife informing me the paramedics were with Sam and he was having a medical emergency. In my mind I was like WHAT! I just spoke with Sam. He sounded good. Now what is going on I was asking myself? So I asked her where he was and where were they taking him. Later I learned that the EMT's staff called the last person that Sam had called on his car redial because his phone required a passcode for use. So apparently his brother was the last person he had spoken to prior to him becoming ill. So I contacted my daughter who lives around the corner from me. She picked me up and when we walked out my front door the police were placing Sam's car in the driveway. When he saw me coming out of the house he asked if I had been in the house all this time and I said "yes." He said he had been ringing the bell but I did not hear anything. So all this was happening in front of my house. Amazingly Sam had made it home from I-95 and apparently rolled onto the lawn of my neighbor who happened to come out that night for a walk. This neighbor informed me later that she normally only walked on Tuesdays and Thursdays and she felt led by the Holy Spirit to go for a walk on that Wednesday evening. So she walked twice around the block and did not see Sam's car there. She was compelled to take an additional walk around the block and on the third time she saw his car on the lawn; and noticed him just sitting in the car. She decided to approach the car because she felt like something was wrong. When she approached the car she noticed the passenger side door was ajar a little so she pulled it opened. When she saw Sam's face, it was obvious he was trying to communicate with his eyes that something was wrong. She immediately called 911 and stayed with him until they arrived. The medical team assessed him and immediately placed him in the ambulance to take him to the nearest hospital.

By now my head is spinning as my daughter and I follow the police officer to the emergency room where I find my husband in the emergency room. He was lying in the bed in major distress, unable to speak although he was conscious, unable to move his right side. The medical staff did a series of assessments and discovered he might be experiencing a TIA which is a small stroke and requested permission to provide treatment. This treatment is crucial and time is of essence so I agreed. Then they discovered, upon the completion of an MRI, that he had a large blood clot on the left side of his brain and needed to be flown to the University of Maryland Medical Center in downtown Baltimore to have it removed immediately. My daughter took me home to change clothes because I knew I was going to be there for some time although not really knowing how this would go. While I was home the surgeon from the University of Maryland called requesting authorization to perform the surgical procedure removing the blood clot from Sam's brain. Of course I consented. After I changed we then proceeded to the hospital. When we arrived they had completed the procedure and my husband was unconscious and in ICU on life support. The neurosurgeon came in to let me know my husband did not have a TIA, but in fact he'd had a massive stroke they diagnosed as terminal. And I was looking at the doctor like absolutely not this can't be. So now it is well after midnight and I am sitting in a chair beside his bed, wondering what in the world was going on. Last week we celebrated our second year of marriage and now the doctor is trying to tell me I may be planning a funeral. Well in my mind this did not add up; it was not making sense to me at all.

So you know what I did. I began asking God what this was!!! I was seeking some answers about what was going on. Conversations with God are often the catalysts for peace in situations that don't yield peace. So I reverted to the conversation I had with God about marrying Sam. I had to remind myself that he had released me to enter this marriage and once I was reminded of that exchange, I was like okay, then what is this? By now I had prayed along with a host of other people who were praying for and with us and in my spirit I felt like everything was going to be alright. I felt God there with us and I kept saying to him, as long as you are with us I know we are good. And I was talking about his manifest presence because he is always with us, but I needed to feel him in that moment, which was my peace in knowing this was going to be good! One very important lesson I have learned from my spiritual dad, Archbishop R. L. Dennis, is not to blame everything on the devil. Surely sickness and disease come from him; however, God has to authorize him to do anything to us. My husband and I are believers and we have faith in God. We had no idea our faith was about to increase tremendously because of this test. Also when I go through things I tend to make assessments to make sure no sin has caused this to fall on us. Are we in right standing with God? After doing all my checks I think we're good. Listen we are not perfect but whatever we struggle with has already been submitted to God so we are covered. So again, "What is this?" I think I must have asked God this question a thousand times before I was able to know how to approach this situation. Although I was clear it would take our faith in God as a healer to see him miraculously move on Sam's behalf.

As the morning rose upon us I was approached by a gang of white coated doctors, ranging from neurosurgeons to neurologists and the primary doctor on Sam's case, a female named Dr. Moss; and they wanted to meet with me about what was happening to him. No bedside manner; very matter-of-fact was their approach. I promise you that I had no idea what I was about to hear but now looking back I was more prepared for that moment than I believed initially. They informed me that my husband had suffered a massive left brain stroke that affected his right side - his speech and the ability to move and function from the right side. They also advised that he would not survive the stroke. Yes they were talking death. They warned me that the blood clot in his brain had caused damage and would eventually cause major swelling. To prevent his skull from crushing due to the swelling they could remove a portion of his skull. Their question for me was whether or not I wanted them to perform that surgery. They quoted a possible 10 percent chance of survival. Or maybe death within four months. And if he lived longer, that he would probably be in a nursing home needing assistance with feeding and dressing. And no speech. I explained in no uncertain terms that I indeed wanted them to perform the surgery to remove his skull so that he could live. They further advised the surgery would not reverse the damage caused by the stroke and they wanted to be sure I understood that almost as if death was their agenda. And I informed them I certainly understood that they could not do anything additionally to help my husband; however I was relying on my faith in God to reverse the damage from the stroke and heal him in ways that

16

exceeded their limitations. The lead physician seemed to grow frustrated with me when I spoke about my faith in God, which caused me to become increasingly frustrated with her. I reminded her that she had no authority over life or death and consequently she was even limited in her knowledge and wisdom; however God is not limited in wisdom or knowledge. I told her my faith is in him and in his ability to move in this place! They made their point and I made mine. Our God reigns even in this and he will get glory with whatever he decides to do. At this point in the matter I was good on the inside. I knew we were in a fight for LIFE literally; not clear as to why, but I was discerning what this was and growing spiritually daily by this event.

So they performed the surgery, removed a portion of Sam's skull and his brain swelled; this was not cute at all and I don't mean cosmetically. I mean this entire situation was horrible, to watch him swell in this manner, then have to wait for the swelling to subside before they could be clear how much damage had been caused by the stroke. I felt like the medical team and I were on opposing teams, as if they wanted to see him die so what they declared would be so. And I definitely wanted him to live so they would understand that God has the final say over his son's life. God caused us to be victorious for sure!

The first couple of days after the surgery he was unconscious and on life support, but I was encouraged because he was breathing 80 percent on his own and only 20 percent on the machine. I would read Psalms 118:17 over Sam multiple times daily. "I will not die, but

17

live and declare the works of the Lord." And I'd pray until heaven came down; my faith was full and I believed God for total recovery. At this point in my life, although I had not experienced anything like this, I had gone through other challenges where I had to exercise my faith against all odds and I watched God turn things around full circle. And although this situation was different, God is the same God and he changes not; he can do anything but fail. I looked at those doctors like we will see who will win this battle. In the meantime I continued to pray and believe God along with a host of other people. My husband and I are loved by many praying people and we have lived off of those prayers. As I continued to pray the doctors continued to bring discouraging news, which was just fuel for me to pray harder and believe more. It was as if something was trying to wear us down; this spiritual warfare was on full stream. Daily they performed neurological tests and initially Sam was responsive. Then one day - I remember like it was yesterday - things began to turn for the worse. He was not responding to any commands, which meant his brain cells were dead. The doctors even took me into a room to show me on a screen that his brain cells had been injured; it looked bad but I could not succumb to that report. I kept saying I cannot receive that, I do not care what the scans showed or the test results displayed; this is all a test and God will show himself strong on our behalf. I kept hearing God say,"This is for my glory." My response was that we are moving forward. At one point the doctor and I argued because she was accusing me of being selfish, wanting Sam to live even if he was not going to have a good quality of life. And I told her not to worry about his quality of life; God had that. I constantly had to tell her to stay in her lane and that she operated from a place of limitations but that our God did not!!!! After having several interactions of this manner, she started avoiding me and that was fine; she didn't have anything good to say anyway and I was tired of hearing her reports. Now initially I knew I needed to hear it so I would know how far God was bringing us from; but on the other hand the bible says faith comes by hearing and hearing by the word of God {*Romans 10:17*} and that's all I wanted to hear to fortify my faith for the foolishness she was speaking. This continued for about two weeks. They then discovered Sam was a retired veteran so they transferred him to the VA hospital. So then we had to deal with a new medical team. I sat in a meeting waiting to hear their assessments. I was already on the defensive. I was ready for them and whatever they had to say. So they gave their report and it was basically the same. He would probably not live long because of the damage, perhaps up to four months and if longer basically in a vegetative state. The devil is a liar. The God I serve loves me and is concerned about everything that is a concern for me and I know this to be the case. Sam's mother responded before I could say anything. She asked them not give up on her son because we were believing God to heal him. The doctor's response was different from the previous physician. He said you are right and I do apologize. So it sounds like this medical team over at the VA at least has some understanding of their limitations and that God could possibly take this on.

This is exactly what happened. The first week Sam was still not responding positively. The neurologist would tell him to do something like raise his hand and Sam would look at him as if he was speaking another language. I continued believing God and encouraging Sam to fight for his life. And it happened on the 29th day of being in the ICU, as if there had been an awakening. The same neurologist came into the room to perform the daily tasks. This day he asked Sam to move his finger and Sam lifted his entire arm up and as the doctor proceeded to leave the room, he turned and looked at Sam and said, "You are going to make a liar out of me." And Sam's mother responded, "He sure is!" From that day we began to see more improvement, so much so that one of the previous doctors responded by saying, "No way. This is unfreaking believable." And my response was, "I told you all that God was going to heal him; and he said, "You sure did." Nothing like sweet victory. Although we still have a long way to go, we have a notable miracle in progress. Yassss miracles, signs and wonders follow them that believe God! Our faith is making us whole. Shortly after that and with more progress, the medical team had to change their direction. They initially were trying to find an assisted living facility for Sam to live out the rest of his days.

But God had other plans. One day one of the nurses told me about the Hunter Holmes McGuire VA Medical Center in Richmond, Va., where they had a polytrauma rehabilitation floor in the hospital. There are only five programs of this type across the country and this was the closest to us. She said Sam was young and that his best chance for maximum recovery would be for us to go there. So I informed the doctors that this is where we wanted to go and they started that process to get him admitted. In the meantime I had to speak with my employer. But they had already extended grace because of the favor of God so I was permitted to work remotely from Richmond while my husband was admitted into the VA Center there. They had the Fisher House for veterans' family members to stay without cost. The accommodations were five star and everyone who knows me knows this was very important to me. This was another assurance that God had us. God had those little details already worked out just for me. During this entire journey we have experienced nothing but the favor of God, which let me know his hand was in it from the beginning and that he was going to work it out in our favor. The fact that Sam made it off of I-95 highway without an accident and made it home for an angel to find him. Surely God was involved in the matter!!!

We were three months into this journey so off to Richmond we went were there for four additional months. I was emotionally drained and exhausted but I felt we were moving forward and God was with us and we are going to be good. So from October to January Sam was in the polytrauma center and I was staying at the Fisher House. He had rehabilitation from 8 a.m. to 4 p.m., so I visited him daily at 4 p.m. until after he ate dinner at 5:30 p.m. because most days he was exhausted because of the rigorous therapy plan they had for him. This schedule worked for me because during the day I was working and when I left him in the evening I was able to get school work completed. I'm still not sure how, but God's grace is sufficient. I also drove home every week to check on the house, get my hair done and show up on site at work to check on things. I would return to Richmond the next day by the time Sam would finish his therapy sessions. We established goals and he was making great strides on his way to being totally independent. The therapist worked him hard every day and Sam gave it 110 percent. God gave grace for healing. Sam had enthusiasm like they had never seen, which was inspiring to the staff and other patients. He would sing to them and they enjoyed his singing. This is amazing because I'm stunned to learn that singing uses a different part of your brain than the portion used for speech.

So Sam was able to learn how to walk again for which I was grateful. I was grateful for every skill he regained, but especially getting out of the wheelchair. It was so hard trying to get it in and out of the car, and then getting him in it. It was horrible for me. I think I cried every time. I am so glad when God released us from that. Sam was so determined. I remember the day they met with us in the hospital and asked if they could install a wheelchair ramp at our home and Sam said "No" emphatically and we all turned to look because he had not been saying much up to this point. The VA told us they had to install it or they would not approve his coming home, so we scheduled the date to have it installed. But by that date Sam was walking into the house, so we canceled that installation. Thank you Jesus!

So he was able to come home for Christmas for a break until the New Year. I soon learned that my new role for my husband was caretaker and I was not ready for this role at all. All I could think was for richer or poorer and in sickness and health. I remember thinking to myself we are declaring restored health as we make it through this sickness. My two-year marriage had succumbed to this. I also remember asking God why not after we had been married for 20 plus years; why not let us build a foundation, and I later learned that this is our foundation and we are building this on solid rock.

When we were preparing to come home, we had to meet with the pharmacist to get the medication list to go home and I promise you my husband must have been on 30 plus medications. I was so emotional, like, Jesus why does he have to take all this medication? So they assured me he would be able to gradually come off most of it and why did they tell me that? Every week I was asking the doctors, "Okay, what medicines are we coming off of this week?" Yes I was my husband's advocate and we not taking all this medication; we are being healed in Jesus' name. So little by little, week by week the medication decreased. Physically, Sam was making progress but the speech was moving rather slowly. He could speak what I now know to be automatic language; phrases like "how are you" and "oh boy," but his struggle is language expression. And sometimes he struggles with comprehension which is called aphasia, something else I had never heard of. All I know is that it all comes from the enemy and we want no parts of it. This right here has an expiration date to it; we may not what the date is but we know it is coming. This was my declaration.

So we came home for Christmas, which everyone knows is my favorite holiday. But this was a special one after all we had been through and I was still in my right mind. I promise you there is a God and I knew he was right there with us. So we were good. We hosted Christmas dinner for both families and it was wonderful. My family teases me because I have had multiple celebrations for Sam coming home and I am going to continue to celebrate this miracle man of mine for life.

In January Sam returned to the University of Maryland to have his skull replaced and I was anxious for the return. I wanted so badly to see the doctors who proclaimed death and/or a vegetative existence over him. I wanted them to see that victory belongs to Jesus and he always delivers. The surgeon came into the room looking like he had seen a ghost. He was genuinely surprised to see Sam in this condition. He sent some of the other members of the original medical team to see him. One of the neurologists said "I don't think I have ever seen anyone recover from such a massive stroke in this manner." I said to one of the doctors, "I told you that God was going to do it and he is not finished yet. We will be back." His response was, "Sometimes you get it right and sometimes you get it wrong." I knew he did not want to believe God did this; he would rather admit that he got it wrong. Either way it spoke to the limitations of physicians. I feel physicians owe it to themselves and their patients to seek a source higher than their level of wisdom and knowledge. That cranioplasty went well as expected and after Sam recovered, he returned to Richmond. But this time he went to their Polytrauma Transitional Rehabilitation Program, which was the next step in his recovery plan. We were six months out and not sure how much longer we had to go, but we still believed God and would not be moved by what had been spoken. We were determined to speak the word of God, allowing him to have the final say. While Sam was in this program they only allowed me to stay for the first two weeks because they did not want family members interfering with the treatment program. This was the next level, getting him prepared to live on his own if he had to. This also gave me an opportunity to rest and replenish myself, which was desperately needed by this time.

Even after six months, I was still expecting this journey to end at every turn and in any moment; but God had another plan. The longer it got the more worn I became. I was starting to see myself in the mirror and I did not want to look myself in the eyes because I was looking worn. I had never experienced anything like this. I had never even seen anyone in my family have to be a caretaker; this was a role far from my resume I assure you. As a caretaker you are intercessor and everything else that is needed. So Sam was there for another four months, still making great strides, except for speech. I was beginning to think there was a conspiracy against his speech; because the physical therapist was a beast but everywhere he had gone for speech was greatly lacking in skills in comparison to his need. My husband was diagnosed with global aphasia with apraxia which in laymen's terms is worst-case scenario. They reported that his speech would not return to normal. My response was that this was the case, so that when God performs this miracle, no one, absolutely no one would be able to say anything other than "this is miraculous." Another notable miracle and we continue to wait and believe God for it! Sam did those four months and returned home for a break. And yes, you've got it. I had another "Sam is coming home" celebration. When he came home he did some speech and physical therapy twice weekly but the speech therapist was horrible and physical therapy reported he had progressed as much as he was going to in that environment.

At this point he is fully independent so even though we are not at total restoration yet, we are a great distance from where we started and definitely far from the diagnosis. I have found no one in the medical path we've followed who has expectations of people getting totally healed. And perhaps this is the case because the medical field needs sick people in its system and I get it; but we will not be a part of this.

So Sam had been home for exactly a year; he needed that time to rest and he no longer wanted to be away from home. Although he was independent, he could not be left alone because he was not able to communicate if there had been an emergency. So part of the week my parents stayed with us and the other days he went to his aunt's house. That got tiring after a while for all parties involved. So we figured it was time to return to

Richmond for additional rehabilitation, especially speech. So he returned for only about 14 weeks this time. During this time there was absolutely no progress. With the VA, as long as there was progress you could stay until you reached your goals, but with no progress, Sam was discharged. In our discharge meeting the therapist gave their reports and basically said Sam has the words in his brain because he was able to repeat words; however he was not retaining the words. They also reported that he could move his right arm, but it was not making a connection to the command center, the brain. This did not discourage me one bit because I felt that as soon as God was ready to release this, it was going to happen. Everything that was needed to make it happen was there, but we needed the miraculous to occur in the brain and God can do it for sure. So we came home and I believe Sam was disappointed not to see any progress this time. I know from my perspective that this had been tough and I can't even begin to imagine from his perspective. But I was encouraged, nonetheless, knowing what our end result would be. God's timing is not our timing but as we wait for our expected end our declaration remains to be total healing and restoration and God always does exceedingly and abundantly above all we can ask or think.

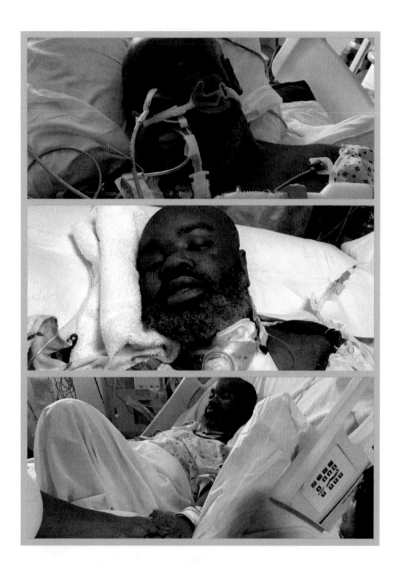

❖   August 25, 2017: On life support.

- ❖ September 9: First day breathing on his own.
- ❖ September 24: Holding hands with his mother and his wife.

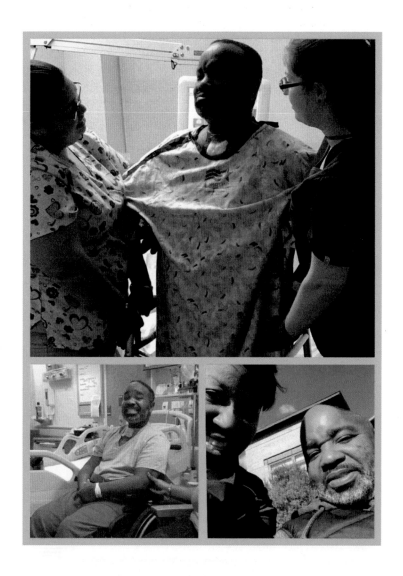

❖ October 16: First day standing.

- ❖ October 21: Arrived in Richmond for therapy.
- ❖ November 4: Enjoying Richmond's balmy weather.

❖ April, 2018: On the way home from Richmond
❖ May 16, 2018: Welcome home party
❖ Elder Sam Stackhouse: Now!!

Chapter four: Making sense of faith

Nothing about faith makes sense. The bible declares faith to be the substance of things hoped for, the evidence of things not seen. {*Hebrews 11:1*} Who hopes for things that you can't see? Well as believers we are all called to have hope in things we cannot see, at least with the natural eye. However it is through our faith that we are able to in time see them unfold. We have to train ourselves to see it before we actually see it! It is in seeing it that we will be able to see it. See? It makes no sense, but it is faith, our fundamental truth as believers. God has given us faith to be able to make the transfer from what we are hoping for even when there is no evidence. Seems to be challenging sometimes until we come to a crossroads in our relationship with God where we have seen enough of him to just have faith for what seems to be impossible. It is based on our experiences with him that our faith grows increasingly for us to have faith for greater things in God. As believers we should always be exercising our faith in God, because there are enough impossibilities in life to keep us on the wheels for faith for life. We all know people who we believe have great faith and we watch them face impossibility after impossibility and we see them become possible. And we are amazed. We can all experience this kind of manifestation in our lives by having the same kind of faith in God.

The bible declares that faith comes by hearing and hearing by the word of God. So if we are desiring to increase our faith we must spend time listening to and reading the word of God. This is how we learn more about who he is and that will increase our confidence in his ability and increase our understanding for his love for us. We have to resist the temptation to doubt not to trust God and the way to doing that is through his word. He has established himself through his word and has even demonstrated that in our lives enough to show that his track record is exemplary. For this very reason once the medical team explained what was going on with my husband, I had no reason to continue hearing it because that could cause me to doubt what God's word says about healing. And because I was exercising my faith I had to rely on God's word; that is what I was believing for. I was declaring life while they were speaking death, and had I allowed them to overshadow my faith, their word could have become a possibility. Now we do not want to ignore reality because that would not be wise, but after we have a full understanding of what is transpiring, then as believers we need to turn to God's prescribed method of operation. And in that we need to understand that there will be opposition, especially when we decide to have faith and trust God in another dimension. We can be assured that opposition will come to discourage us and we have to be determined to be encouraged despite what the adversary tries to bring against us. We have the assurance that our faith in God, who is all knowing, will move on our behalf without fail. Faith does not mean that God always does what we want him to do. Our faith has to be matured in God and we have to know that God is God regardless of what he does. And I had to get myself in the place that if God had decided to end Sam's life in those moments, this did not mean that God is not good. God is good when things turn out how we desire and when they do not. That requires a certain level of maturity in God otherwise we become fair weather believers in God. He is not our magician to move at our every beck and call. He is our loving father who has an intent for our lives; and when the enemy comes against that, he will do battle on our behalf. This flows out of our relationship with God and without that, life is more challenging than it needs to be.

We need to surrender and submit to God's will for our lives and understand this is not about our plan for our life. When we view God as the creator that he is, we understand that his intent for our lives is more important than any plans we could ever desire. Our trust for him allows us to seek him for his plan, and surrender to that plan, taking it on and moving in that direction. Be obedient to what he is requiring. It takes courage to be obedient; however when we are reliant upon God, knowing he cares for us and the things that are a concern for us, it becomes easier. The more we mature in God the more we seek his will and desire, understanding that to be most important.

Our maturity also causes us to be able to rest in God because we understand he has us. In past times I have wondered how some people can go through things that seemed tumultuous and have such a peace on them that only comes from resting in God. Most times in this journey I have been able to rest in God and the times that I have become anxious and unsure were the times I was relying on myself and not allowing the rest of God to consume me. Some of my own anxiety was due to my wanting things to happen according to my timeline as well, not fully understanding that God knows what he is doing. And my not seeing him move did not mean he was not moving. So what do we do in the delay, which is really determined by our perception of the delay? What does the delay mean for our situation? And in most cases God is silent during the delay. What is our response to the silence and what does it mean? Everything is determined by our interpretation of the two. How we define them dictates how we respond or even our lack of response.

What we think is a delay is God moving according to his timing, not ours, because he is in control. Also God moving behind the scenes, moving things we have yet to discern. If not cautioned in the delay, we sometimes allow doubt to overshadow us and then fear and anxiety creep in. It is crucial to remain in faith that keeps us in the rest of God, knowing that even in the lapse of time between what has occurred and what we are believing God for, it will happen. Make sure you are connected to people who have faith and sometimes that can be difficult even among believers. We all have different measures of faith and sometimes what you are believing God for is impossible for others to see. This journey has been interesting. When I speak what we are believing God for to some believers, the responses we have gotten have been intriguing, to say the least. When nonbelievers respond with disbelief that is the appropriate response; however when people who proclaim to know God respond in the same manner, it is mind blowing. No matter how mind blowing it is, I have not been persuaded otherwise; it has just been duly noted. This is why it is key for you to know what you believe. And no matter who stands with you, knowing on some days you may stand alone and that will have to be enough for you; stand flat footed with no equivocation. At all cost, stand in faith believing and your faith will deliver that for which you have believed. Your faith may cost relationships, causing you to be isolated; as long as God is with you this is a good place for you to be. God knows what you need and when you need it.

Sensory perception versus faith: we are so accustomed to living in the natural that if things do not measure up to our senses we find them hard to believe. Meaning, if we are not able to see it with our eyes, feel it through touch, even smelling it, hearing it or tasting it, this poses a problem for some of us. As believers we are called upon to be spiritual beings and live our lives spiritually discerning things versus naturally discerning them.

HERE!!!!!Faith is not faith until it's been tested. We make declarations and proclaim ourselves as believers and when life happens and it happens to us all that will be the determining factor as to how much faith really exist. God does allow situations to occur in our lives to increase our faith even in times when we feel like it is too much at the end of the matter we discover that it was in us all along. God knows what He has placed inside of us and we are more prepared for the battle than we know however we do find that to be the case in the end. God also knows what kind of pressure is required to bring it out of us. This is not the kinds of things we like to discuss but God does allow us to be crushed and His intent is never to harm us but to bring out of us that which He placed inside of us. In those times faith is required because in our emotions we can become angry with God for allowing this to happen. I know I am speaking truth because in my own life I have had to pray asking God to keep my heart from hardening especially when we consider God can keep all of this away from us but that does not mature us and grow us in Him. He is concerned about those things that concern us but ultimately it is about our development in Him so some pain He will not spare us from although He could and for some people that is a hard pill to swallow.

I remember being in a real bad place as it relates to Sam being sick but I was pushing my way through it still coming to worship and I remember hearing someone say who worships a God who will not finish the miracle and I thought great question. As I continued on through this journey my answer to that question is the person who believes that He is not finished yet and although there has been a delay and although He has been quiet all I got is my faith in this place without it I am done! This is my understanding of Faith making me whole because most days I understood that without it I was a disaster waiting to happen which is what the enemy wanted. The enemy of my soul wanted no only to kill Sam but destroy me in any way that he could which made me that much more determined to press into God especially on the hard days. Who gets married to have their husband suffer a stroke that leaves him not able to speak to me that was crazy and it had to be more to this situation. All I have is my faith and I believe that is all we need to see the manifestation of our miracle. And I promise you that God is faithful miracles still happen every day! For those who believe that God does not perform miracles today shame on you however for me I want to continue to see the manifestation of miracles and I have the faith for it given to me by Almighty God. Yes He equipped me for this journey as stated previously more than I fully understood. You never go through things without coming out on the other side of it changed never to be the same. My convictions are stronger

And faith has been endowed and I am more committed to believing God and encouraging those who have lost faith or belief in God to have the courage to believe and have Faith again!!!

Miracles, signs, and wonders follow them that believe and we believe God and a few miracles signs and wonders that follow us. Miracles are the temporary suspension of the natural order of events or the reversal of natural laws. Nature has laws that are set in motion that when certain things occur then other things follow however God has supernatural laws that at His ordering can and will cause an interruption to the natural law. It don't make sense and scratch our heads when they occur because although we believe God for them we never fully understand how it happens. Those are the mysteries of God and He will forever keep us confounded if we dare to believe. I do not want to just read about the miracles that are written in the word of God I want to be used of God for Him to perform the miraculous in the earth realm today causing others to believe in Him and others to believe in Him again!

Chapter Five: I have found grace to be amazing!

It was his grace! His grace is everything. I have found grace to be amazing. The word declares that God's grace is sufficient and I have found that to be the case. When I was immature I thought grace was God's way of covering our sins, and as I matured in him I discovered that when I received his sanctifying grace it gave me the strength I needed to not live in sin. Then as I matured even more I learned that with grace comes enabling power and strength to get things accomplished, which is serving grace. Whatever assignment or task God was requiring of me, I now understood I had the grace to get it done. It makes difficult things appear effortless even when you know it is difficult. Walking through this journey I am clear that the grace of God rests on my life in ways that have unfolded throughout this journey. The fact that I was able to make it through and remain in my right mind despite the crushing that I felt in my spirit; it was his grace. My husband coming close to death after only two years of marriage was weighing on my psyche and I realized wives have buried husbands in less time and my prayers went out to them. This helped me to better understand that it was his grace. Even the fact that I had become his caretaker, I thought this is not the way this was supposed to turn out. So I grabbed hold to his grace. Clearly he had a portion for me that I was not even aware of and I found it every time I needed it. I was able to keep up with my job and they were amazed that I was able to keep everything going. It was his grace. On top of that I was able to complete my doctoral degree despite the fact that my dissertation chairperson thought I should take a semester or two off. I had a finishing spirit on the inside of me that kept me pushing and I was glad that I did. When I walked across the stage to get that degree I knew God had ordained this very thing for my life, because it was his grace that kept me pushing through it all. The fact that my husband suffered the stroke only 45 days after we settled on our new home and although we lost income we were able to pay all our bills on time. This is the grace and favor of God. I was able to decorate our new home through this process; the retail therapy helped me as well. I understand well that God's hand is on both Sam's and my life and he orchestrated our introduction and union and today I am more clear about that than I have ever been. I have felt his hand involved in this entire journey giving me strength to continue even on the bad days and there were many. The grace of God covered me, making it appear as if it was nothing, but I assure you there were days I almost lost it…I felt like my mind was playing tricks on me. However it was his grace that would not allow me to lose it because he has a plan for us and we are moving forward in that journey despite the enemy's attempt. It will not prosper. And because of his grace this will all work out for our good. We are witnesses in the earth of a gracious God who shows mercy to those he chooses.

Now I know why the psalmist sang amazing grace because it certainly is and has been amazing in my life prior to this point and more evident now because I have said in this journey right here it has been awful and amazing all at the same time. It was awful that we had to experience this, but we have gotten to know God in new ways because of this experience. I am clear that I could have had to bury my husband and there were some who thought that was going to be the case, but his grace and mercy kept us moving forward. I kept reminding myself that we were passing through this place; we are not staying here and as we continued to progress I just kept saying it was his grace that is keeping us. Yes the grace of God has keeping power along with the ability to accomplish the unthinkable.

Chapter six: 'I will do a new thing,' says the Lord

*Forget about the former things I'm doing something new
don't you perceive it or know it?*
Isaiah 43:18-19

A lot of us feel like we know God based on how he has moved in our lives. Those experiences cause us to become familiar with who he is and how he operates; however we really only know God based on those experiences we have had with him. Just in the same manner that we become familiar with our family and friends and others we come into contact with. For instance, if we have experienced sickness and God has healed us, we can say I know God to be healer. If we have experienced the provision of God then we come to know him as a provider. All the knowledge we have about God is based on our occurrences and the more we experience with him, the more we grow and mature in our understanding of him and who he is. God uses challenges in our lives, the things the enemy throws our way to make us stumble, and even the challenges we cause ourselves to mature us in him. He desires for us to know him more intimately and with every level of challenge we become more familiar.

So we know God but we do not know God. We sometimes resist getting to know God in new ways because we have become complacent in our familiarity with God. We become accustomed to the ways he's moved previous seasons and that gives us a certain level of comfort. We get relaxed with God and his ways; we become complacent in that knowledge of God even though we know there is so much more to who God is. It is something about us being comfortable and not really wanting to be stretched; although our declaration is that we want to go to the next level our actions rarely align. And instead of having that "Peter in the boat" experience with God...where he asked Jesus to bid him come out of the boat and step onto the water. This is uncomfortable for some of us and we would rather remain in a place that is safe because we are acquainted with our current location. Being familiar brings us a certain level of peace and puts us at ease because we feel we have a certain level of control. In familiar situations we feel like we know what the outcome will be and that gives us a level of assurance which is contrary to faith. Peter had another level of faith in God, not knowing what would happen once he stepped out of the boat. I believe he had confidence that Jesus would keep him safe even if the experience was a new one; he was willing to move forward to know and learn something about Jesus.

Yes God desires to do a new thing in us all. He asks whether we perceive what it is he is trying to do in our lives that is different from previous times. God desires us to know him, and in knowing him we have to have new and different experiences that will sometimes be uncomfortable and unfamiliar for us. The new thing that God desires to do in us challenges, stretches and ultimately matures us in ways we have not formerly known ourselves to be. God has a purpose for the stretching and that will not be experienced in our comfort zones.

Perhaps it is fear and anxiety that prevents us from desiring the new things God wants to do and being in the unfamiliar makes us very uncomfortable. We do not like being uncomfortable even to get to the next level. We want to reach our goals effortlessly. We want to stay in the comfort zone because it is safe, so we tell ourselves. We are not sure what the unfamiliar will cost us, knowing that it will cost us something; however it is the price we pay in exchange for a new experience with God, which is ultimately priceless. It will cost us some relationships, reputation, finances, our own will and desires; but the trade-off is allowing God to have his way in our lives, which should be our main focus. What God exchanges in our lives for the sacrifices we make is really an uneven exchange and for that we should be grateful.

What are we afraid of? God is constantly beckoning us on to greater because he placed greater inside us when he made us; nevertheless we desire to remain in a place of comfort when there is so much new territory to cover with God.

So our knowledge of God is limited although God is not limited. We know him only according to our last experience with him. He desires our knowledge of him to be ever growing and expanding. There is so much of him to discover and this journey is planned and designed for us that we only have to follow into new territory, which makes most of us very uncomfortable. Sometimes we have to have the courage to go with him anyway, even if we are afraid; and the more experiences we have with him, the more our faith and trust in him is increased so we know he has us and all that concerns us.

The Father is always bidding us to seek him and that door is open to us constantly so that we can have new experiences with him. He created us in this fashion but somehow we have allowed other desires that we believe to be more pertinent than the desire to seek him a priority. Somehow he gets placed after everything else when our only focus in life should be the search to really know him. In this we would discover that if we would seek him, we could avoid chasing after things that are not for us.

We seek to know a lot of things and people we think will advance our cause. We place emphasis on networking to know people who we deem as important and who we think will get us into places we desire to be. When the only person we need to seek to know more is God, who is a master at making the kinds of connections we need with the right people.

We seem to think we know what is best for our lives better than the One who created us in his image and for his purpose. We need to lean in and pursue him more. We have wasted time trying to figure out our own lives when there is already a master blue print we can access to follow. Our actions seem like we are trying to figure things out when life could be simpler doing it the way God designed it.

The psalmist David questioned who we are that God Almighty would be mindful of us. Well he knows us and in our discovery of who he is helps us know who we are because we only find that in him. It is impossible to discover who we are outside of God because who we are is only found in him. Some of us are on a quest to discover who we are outside of him and just as we will not fully know who God is outside of seeking him, we will not become fully aware of who we are until we seek him.

It is amazing that in seeking him, not only is he revealed, but who we are in him is revealed as well. All that we are, who he created us to be, our gifts and talents are all wrapped up in the one who created us. This is crucial because this shows we could never be a full expression of ourselves without him and we certainly try. That means we could be so much greater seeking him regularly; not just when we find ourselves in trouble, but before that so we might not find ourselves in trouble. In our seeking we discover he has a plan that leads us through those troubled waters and the knowledge gained through the process now expands our knowledge of him. Again. Knowing him does not exempt us from trouble; however knowing him guarantees our successes and victories with whatever we face.

God loves us and we are not always mindful that he created us for his own pleasure; but we are forever trying to remain on our own agenda instead of following his plan. It seems life would be much simpler if we followed his leading not only when it is convenient but all the time at all cost. We need to fully understand that the life he has designed for us is far greater than anything we could ever have devised for ourselves.

Seeking him would save us so much heartache and frustration along with time. There are traps and ensnarements that have been designed by the enemy to look appealing to us; but our seeking of God would allow us to see things for what they really are and help us avoid those traps.

The more we seek God, the more experiences we have with him, the more we know him in intimate ways. He is always calling us away to spend time with him. He is always trying to reveal himself in ways we cannot even imagine, but it makes us uncomfortable and is frightening for a lot of us. It also makes us feel like we are not in control and that brings anxiety, not knowing what will happen. This is why we have to trust God even in new territory we have to be confident in his ability to keep us safe through it all. Trusting God comes only through knowing him and that should be constantly growing. God is forever moving and we sometimes fail to move with him, causing us to miss what he is doing in our lives.

We really do not want to be where God moved last but where he is moving currently. Where is God trying to take you? What is God trying to do in your life but you've not trusted him enough to make that move? In

Isaiah 43 he ask after saying I will do a new thing, do you not perceive it and for most of us we do but it's scary so you act like you don't perceive it. Comfort zones are the worst it causes us to forfeit the new things that God desires to do then we become frustrated about not moving along in life but it is at our own doing. God is beckoning us into new territory but our own will keeps us from moving forward.

Let us make this move together allowing God to have his perfect will in our lives. Sometimes we have to allow ourselves to become so desperate for him that we have enough courage to overcome fear and anxiety to make the leap into seeking God following his uniquely designed path for our lives even when things do not appear to us to be lined up.

Let us not be so arrogant as to think we know what is best for our lives, more than the one who created us. Life would be so much better with a constant flow of seeking and following after his leading of course. We have to be mindful that every new level starts in a space that is unfamiliar to us, but as we seek God and God reveals himself to us, we are learning the new place God has us in. Sometimes there is no precedence, nothing for us to follow, no footsteps from a previous journey and it can be intimidating. We might have had confidence in the last place, but in the new place we have to become totally reliant upon God again because we do not recognize this place. In the new place we have to surrender and submit to a whole new pattern of being and doing, because the old ways will not secure our victory in this new place. God is helping us develop new patterns and ways of being in this new place that will yield another dimension in him, causing our faith to unfold, displaying that which we have not seen before. Transformation is taking place in this new place and as we come to know God differently, another part of who we are is also being revealed.

We have to be confident in the God that we have surrendered our hearts too, believing that no matter what he allows life to bring, ultimately he has a plan for us to be victorious on the other side of it. We have to know and believe in our hearts that we always win and we have to be careful of what declarations we make, because assuredly we will have to align our words with our actions. Time out for saying,"I have faith in God," and when something happens to test that faith, there is a great distance between the declaration and the action being displayed in the moment. There is a saying that faith is not faith until it has been tested. As Christians, we destroy our witness when we speak about our faith then fall apart during testing time. Faith is supposed to be displayed for others to see because that is how we are able to be great witnesses in the earth of who God is. He works in and through us and what comes out of our mouth should be aligned with our walk.

So as we are walking in this new season we are surrendered and submitted to God for his leading into the plan he has for our lives. It is both exciting and frightening because of the unknown; however what we do know is that God has been and always will be faithful. And that remains to be our declaration despite the road we are traveling. We trust God in every way we know and rely on him for guidance and peace as he leads.

Chapter Seven: Perfect Conditions

Sometimes in life things are not always going to seem like the best conditions to start something new, to branch out or moving into unfamiliar territory. Based on the circumstance you find yourself in, it may appear that things are over for you; that this is the ending when in reality it really is just the beginning of something being orchestrated by God. You may feel like you should pack up and call it quitting time, but I want to caution you to look a little deeper into who is guiding you. How you have gotten into this place where you find yourself pondering what is happening or even why this is occurring. The kinds of questions that we ask ourselves when we are unsure of things after they have become haywire. When things seem to be out of order, this is the best time to give way to a new order of things. In times like these God moves and operate in his own agenda and although it can be frightening not knowing what will occur in the unfamiliar place, it can be an exciting time as you launch out into deep waters with him as your guide.

While on this journey, God has made it clear that he desires to do a new thing in our lives and although we thought we had an understanding; we discover he is detouring us off our route to place us on his route. Clearly God was interrupting our lives through this debacle causing our attention to be fully focused on him and what his desire is for our lives. Nothing like something that shakes your world, even your very existence to the core, to help put everything into perspective. Things that seemed very important became minute in the scheme of things, and somehow things that seemed very small now overshadow everything else. Life has a way of bringing everything together after outwardly tearing it all apart. One thing I have learned is that it is all about perspective; how you view something definitely determines your attitude which ultimately has a major impact on outcome. After all, the outcome establishes what happens next on the agenda.

While watching the funeral of President George H. W. Bush, one interesting fact that resonated with me was his use of the military acronym CAVU, which stands for "ceiling and visibility unlimited" as his approach to everything he faced in life. This is the description of perfect flying conditions. He was one to assess the situation prior to deciding to launch anything. Once I heard this, I could not release it. I was inclined to believe he was speaking about all conditions being clear to move forward with whatever task he was planning to take on. A wise method, otherwise you could be met with major obstacles in adverse conditions. I am not inclined to believe that all conditions need to be perfect; however, that can also depend on your outlook on the matter.

Adverse conditions, situations and circumstances can exist originally to be stumbling blocks, something to deter one from moving forward without opposition. Sometimes the opposition is sent to bring out the press inside of you that is needed to get to the desired place. However without the right perspective and the press, one will never know what is possible and might miss out on an opportunity of a life time all because conditions were not perfect. Adverse conditions sometimes create resistance and resistance combined with both perspective and determination create momentum that cannot be stopped.

In Philippians we are encouraged to press towards the mark of the high calling in Christ Jesus. This message was given to us because God knew that conditions would not be always be perfect, but that we needed to find a way to move forward, to push past the opposition to reach the call that is higher than us all. Think about all the people who decide not to push forward because of less than perfect conditions, never reaching the higher limits that was established for them by God. It takes courage to move against what may seem like impossibilities and challenges that may appear permanent, only to discover that once you get to the other side what has been accomplished is something indescribable. God never leads us into places that are impossible; however he does lead us into places that cause us to stretch beyond ourselves. In this place we have to become totally reliant on him to move past unfavorable conditions but with Him all things are possible.

Resistance is defined as the refusal to accept or comply with something; the attempt to stop something by action or argument. This is what the enemy tries to do in our lives and we should become accustomed to his antics because they are not new. He creates adverse conditions like road blocks to try and stop us from moving forward. As we mature in God we understand his ways and know that on the other side of the press exist the conditions that are needed to operate in the desired place. We have to be so determined to allow nothing to keep us out of the will of God, knowing that if he has established this for our lives he has also equipped us to move forward according to his plan. And this is how we approach purpose for our lives; we go after it with all we have inside us, knowing that victory is ours.

We have spiritually discerned that ceiling and visibility are unlimited for us to move forward in birthing LIFE ministries. This is our perspective. Others looking into our situation may consider the conditions not ideal based on their perspective. After you have sought God for direction for your life and godly counsel because God does instruct us to do so, it is important that you move in the direction God is moving you toward. Ultimately we are being held accountable for our own lives and no one else will have to give an account on our behalf.

There is a certain level of peace that exists when moving out into a new place even when conditions are not perfect, but knowing God is with you provides a certain level of assurance that all things will work together for your good. God is faithful and keeps his promises to his children. His reputation precedes him and this also gives us confidence in moving forward. It has been my experience that when you move forward, God has a way of changing conditions, making them favorable for you. So. Make your move!

In closing...

Just know that God uses everything that we face in life for an opportunity for growth and spiritual development. When we face situations that brings us to our knees we need to fully understand there is where He wants us. As we mature in Him we learn to seek Him especially in those moments of fear and uncertainty. Remember that our faith in God is the key to manifestation and in most cases we are not able to make sense of it at all. We will always wonder how God will work this out and it is never according to our methods or timing. God is sovereign and our trust for Him yields us the peace we need to allow Him the space and time to do what He promises to do in our lives. Every single time we have needed God He has proven Himself to be faithful by coming through and as we look back over our lives this remains to be truth. God has placed us in the earth with a purpose in mind and we ought to seek after that purpose because without actualizing that a problem in the earth is awaiting its solution. We have to know that adversity will surely come however we are equipped to overcome and be victorious indeed!

Nothing is a surprise to God He is all knowing and ever present with wisdom and knowledge that supersedes all knowledge and wisdom in the earth. So when we seek Him for guidance and direction we are assured to be headed in the right direction without failure. And even when we face interruptions in life we understand that it is at His allowance and although in those times of uncertainty we find peace in knowing that He has us covered. Having faith in God is being able to hope for something that there may be no evidence for however as we believe God and He manifest Himself this increases our faith in Him for greater. Yes our faith in God grows and develops which allows us to see impossibilities become possible. And whatever God is calling us to do it is possible and He has given us the grace to complete every assignment in our lives regardless of the challenges that may exist. So we must allow God to do the new thing in our lives without resistance or hesitation knowing that we are in good hands with Him. We cannot allow fear of the unfamiliar or wanting to remain in our comfort zones to allow us to forfeit the next move of God. God desires to take us higher in Him and His plans for our lives are good even when we experience adverse conditions. We have to know that He will use those conditions to develop us into who He has created us to be. So if the conditions are not perfect that does not necessarily mean that this is not God perhaps God is redirecting you on to another path that aligns with His desire for your life but you have to be willing to seek hard after Him. You will find God in the hard places in life and know that He is right there fighting with and for you ensuring that you have the victory as promised. With this who hesitates to have Faith in a God who proves Himself daily allow every situation that comes in your life to be the catalyst that establishes you on the path of destiny for your life. A life lived in purpose is our ultimate goal; anything short of that should not be acceptable.

Meet the Author

Dr. Toni Boulware Stackhouse...

...is the co-founder of LIFE Ministries alongside her husband Elder Samuel Andrew Stackhouse III. She is a Licensed Clinical Professional Counselor for the state of Maryland. Her passion for ministry is outreach and this passion extends to the marketplace where she has been serving those experiencing homelessness in many different capacities for the last twenty years. During this time she has also provided extensive work in mental health and substance abuse. Dr. Stackhouse has a Doctor of Education Degree in Counseling Psychology from Argosy University, a master's degree in Human Services with a concentration in counseling from Lincoln University, a bachelor's degree in Organizational Leadership from Nyack College, and an associates of arts degree in Human Services from the Community College of Baltimore County.

Dr. Stackhouse has great faith in God and demonstrates that faith in her obedience to God's word. In Isaiah 43:19 God says, *"Behold, I will do a new thing; now it shall spring forth; shall ye not know it? I will even make a way in the wilderness, and rivers in the desert."* In this season of her life she is watching God manifest himself in the new thing! Dr. Stackhouse describes herself as a woman who believes God and the scripture that declares miracles, signs and wonders follow them that believe. The LIFE that God is allowing her to live is transformation at its best, and she's trading nothing for her journey! She is a teacher, preacher, intercessor, mentor, coach, workshop presenter and author.

Dr. Toni and Elder Samuel Stackhouse are parents to Trenae L. Watson and her husband, Arlen and Marcus Stackhouse. They also have two grandsons AJ and Ayven. In their spare time they love traveling and spending time with family and friends.

Made in the USA
Middletown, DE
25 August 2019